Behavior Charts

and beyond...

simple, handmade charts that work!

By Tracy Milanese, MS

The author can be contacted at tlmilanese@gmail.com

Cover drawings by my daughter,
Charlotte Milanese, age 6.

Book Design by Tracy Milanese and
Longfeather Book Design
LongfeatherBookDesign.com

ISBN 978-0615708584

DEDICATION

To the people God placed in my life who taught me that a fun approach to teaching kids produces the best results!

Table of Contents

Introduction

THIS BOOK WAS DESIGNED for caregivers who are struggling with varieties of oppositional behavior in children. Behavior charts have been shown to help reduce or eliminate many unwanted behaviors and can be easy and fun to use. Throughout this book caregivers can learn how to make and implement many fun behavior charts for kids in their care.

STEPS TO SUCCESS

1.  "I don't want Susie leaving a wet towel on the floor anymore."

The first step in starting a chart program is to identify the undesirable behavior. It would be best to work on one target behavior at a time

2.  "Susie, I would like you to hang up your towel from now on and I will hang a reminder for you to see."

Let the child know what the expectation is by verbally telling the child and having it posted somewhere for her to see.

3. 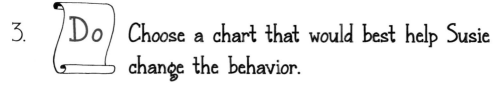 Choose a chart that would best help Susie change the behavior.

Tell the child that you are going to help her change that behavior by using a chart and explain how it will work.

Once the chart is selected and made, the changes can

begin. Hang it in a convenient location where the child can see it often. Be consistent and use it for a period of time before changing it. Remember, charts are only a tool. Children change the quickest when they have a genuine interest in the program and a genuine connection with their caregiver.

Behavior Charts

and beyond...

Get Dressed Chart

Materials
- poster board
- laminated construction paper
- velcro

How to Make
- Draw an outline of a child on poster board.
- Cut clothing (and accessories) out of construction paper (laminate if possible).
- Affix velcro to the backs of clothing and corresponding places on the outline.
- Create a basket with an opening on top out of brown construction paper and attach to the poster board.

How to Use
- This chart is used for younger children who need encouragement to get dressed independently. Each time he dresses himself, he can put a piece onto the outline. When all of the pieces are put on the chart, he receives a reward.
- A second use is to have the child get dressed with the picture. When the child puts his shirt on, he can also put the shirt up on the chart and continue until he is fully dressed.

Best Age Group
3-6 years

Get Dressed Chart

Fill a Paper Plate

Materials

- paper plates
- stickers

How to Make

- Have a paper plate and a supply of stickers in a convenient location.

How to Use

- This is used for younger children who will be rewarded with earning the stickers themselves. As the child picks up his toys or completes other tasks, he is able to pick a sticker and put in on his paper plate. He is able to see how many stickers he has at the end of each day.

Best Age Group

3-6 years

Fill a Paper Plate

Fill Up the Jar

Materials

- baby food jar
- small candies

How to Make

- Set the baby food jar in view in a designated area.
- Have small candies handy.

How to Use

- Each time the child demonstrates a desired behavior, a candy is dropped into his jar for him to see. At the end of the day, he can have the contents of the jar.

Best Age Group

5-9 years

Puzzle Chart

Materials

- a copy of something the child likes (cartoon character, superhero, etc)
- piece of card board the same size

How to Make

- Cut the picture into about 20 puzzle pieces or less.
- Make a corresponding grid on cardboard for each piece to fit, then number the pieces.

How to Use

- Each time the child completes the desired behavior, he gets one piece of the puzzle put in place. When he completes the puzzle, he receives a reward.

Best Age Group

5-10 years

Puzzle Chart

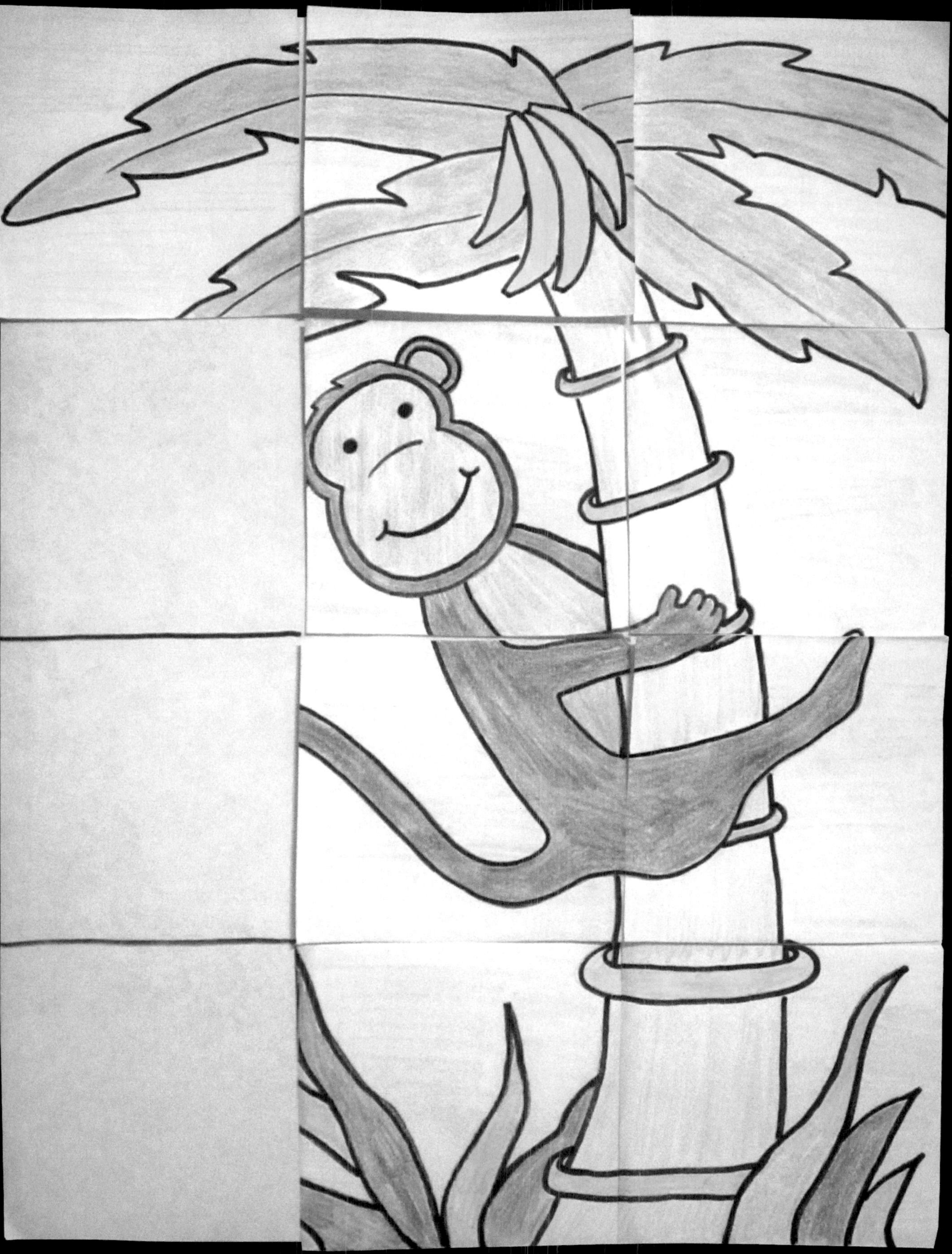

Sibling Chart

Materials
- foam board
- change (pennies, nickels, dimes, quarters)
- tape

How to Make
- Draw an outline of something each sibling likes on the foam board.
- Have pocket change handy.

How to Use
- Each time siblings show positive behavior toward one another such as sharing, helping each other, talking nicely, etc, they receive a coin taped up on their shape. When both shapes are full, they get to count and keep the money.

Best Age Group
5-10 years

Sibling Chart

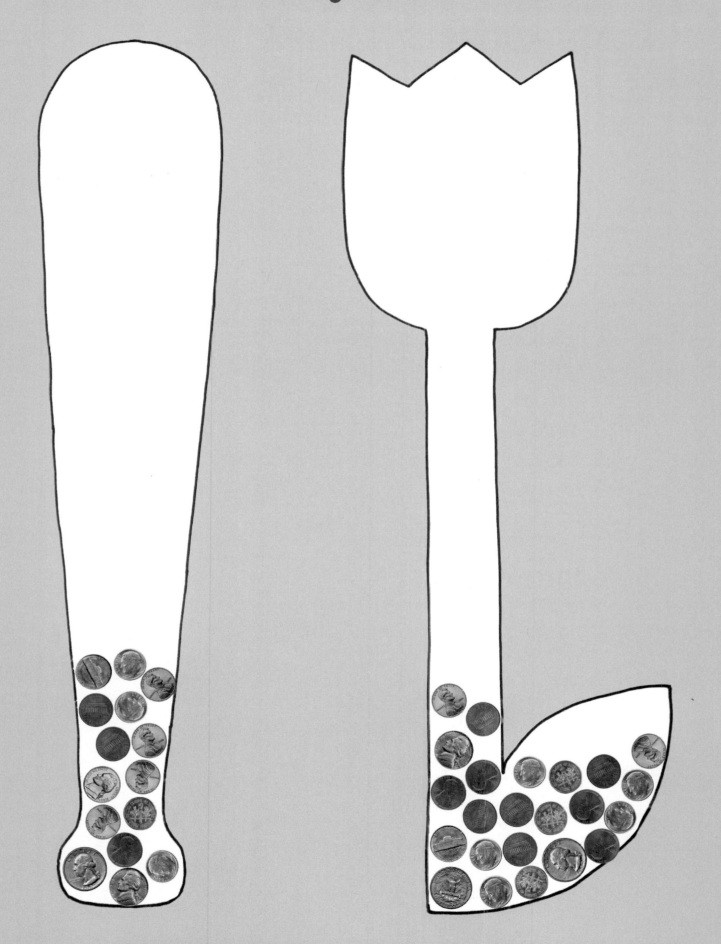

Gameboard Chart

Materials

~ old gameboard + game piece

~ wire

~ duct tape

How to Make

~ Attach wire to the back of an old gameboard with duct tape and hang in a convienient location.

~ Affix game piece to the board at "start" position using duct tape.

How to Use

~ When the child completes a desired behavior, he moves ahead one space. He wins the game when he crosses the finish line. He may also receive a treat or privilege at this point.

Best Age Group

5-10 years

Gameboard Chart

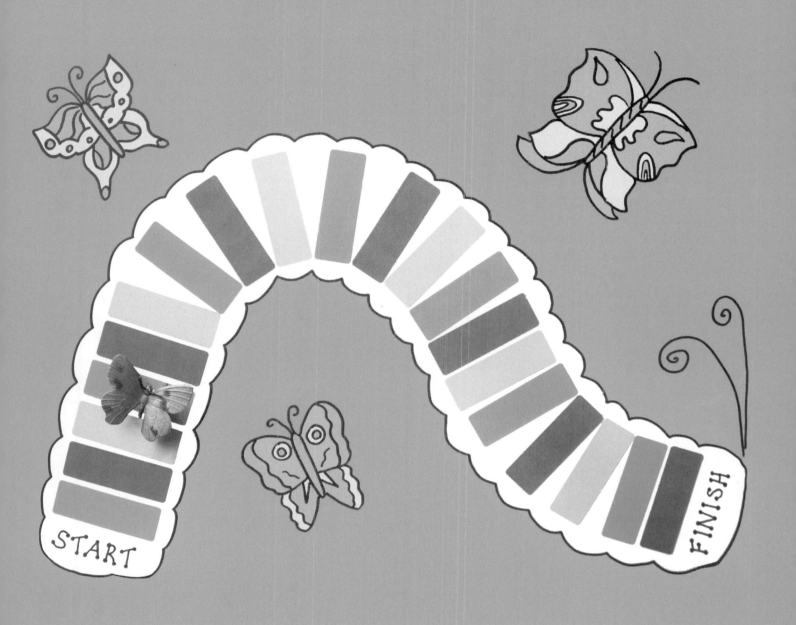

Favorite Food Chart

Materials

- poster board

- markers/crayons

- velcro

How to Make

- Draw and cut out a large food item that has small pieces such as a pizza with toppings or an ice cream cone with sprinkles. The small items must be made separately.

- Attach velcro to the backs of the (10-12) small items and to the large item.

How to Use

- This chart was designed for picky eaters or those with behaviors related to meal times. Each time the child demonstrates desired behaviors around mealtime he gets to put a "topping" on the food chart. When it is filled he can pick a meal or dessert to have that week.

Best Age Group

5-10 years

Favorite Food Chart

What Did I Do Today? Chart

Materials
- posterboard
- velcro
- markers

How to Make
- Hang a poster board and attach 8-12 pieces of velcro spaced apart.
- Write activities on index cards and put velcro on the backs of each.
- Create a pocket by folding up the bottom part of the posterboard write "WHAT DID I DO TODAY?" on the pocket.

How to Use
- This chart is made to keep track of things such as schoolwork, chores or leisure activities. Many children do better if they can see the expectations or choices they have. When used for leisure activities, it helps the child engage in a variety of activities. If used for school work or chores, it helps him see what he has accomplished and what he has left to do. The child simply removes a card from the chart and puts it into the pocket as he completes it. He can receive a reward when all of the assignments are finished.

Best Age Group
5-10 years

What Did I Do Today? Chart

Open the Door Chart

Materials

- 2 pieces of poster board or an old advent calendar

- markers

How to Make

- Use an old advent calendar and add desired pictures inside the windows. Or:

- Attach two pieces of poster board around the edges and cut flaps that open and close.

- Affix pictures/words or rewards behind each window.

- Draw an outline of a school, store, or house around the window flaps.

How to Use

- This chart can be used in two ways. One way is to place different words or pictures of rewards behind each window. At the end of the day if the child has completed all desired tasks, he can choose a window to open and receive that reward.

- It can also be used as a fun daily schedule for chores or schoolwork. The child can choose any door to open and complete whatever is behind the door. This can create an adventure out of an everyday schedule.

Best Age Group

5-10 year

Open the Door Chart

Daily Schedule

Materials

- copy paper
- copier/printer

How to Make

- Create a daily schedule by hand or computer (may need slight change each day).
- Create two columns with a happy face above one and a sad face above the other.

How to Use

- Each morning the child is given a schedule for that day. As he completes a task he can have a happy face or a sad face depending on how the task as completed. A number of happy faces is needed to earn a reward for that day.

Best Age Group

5-10 years

Daily Schedule

name _____

breakfast

brush teeth

get dressed

piano practice

school

lunch

school

outside play

supper

shower

brush teeth

bedtime

Plant a Garden

Materials
- cardboard flat
- dirt
- plastic wrap
- craft sticks
- construction paper
- tape

How to Make
- Fill the cardboard flat with dirt.
- Cover with plastic wrap.
- Make flowers or vegetables out of construction paper and tape to the craft sticks.

How to Use
- Each day the child completes a specific goal he is able to plant something in his garden. When the garden is full, he receives a reward or privilege.

Best Age Group
5-10 years

Plant a Garden

Ladder Chart

Materials
- poster board or cardboard
- photo of child
- velcro
- picture of reward

How to Make
- Create a ladder shape out of the poster board.
- Cut out a photo of the child + affix velcro to the back.
- Affix a piece of velcro to each rung on the ladder.
- Hang a picture of the reward at the top of the ladder.

How to Use
- Place the photo of the child at the bottom of the ladder. As the child completes a desired behavior he moves up a rung. When he reaches the top he receives the reward.

Best Age Group
5-12 years

Ladder Chart

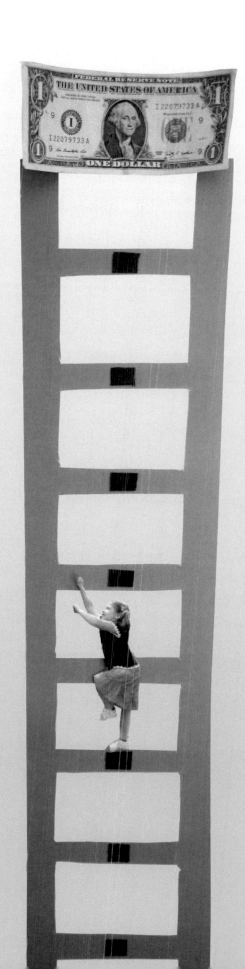

Treasure Map Chart

Materials

- poster board

- markers

- plastic baggie or waterproof box

- velcro

How to Make

- Create a treasure map on the poster board using real landmarks.

- Cut a foot out of the poster board and attach velcro along the path of the map.

- Hide a real treasure inside the baggie or box and bury it, mark the spot with an X.

How to Use

- As the child completes the desired task he can move his foot one step on the path. When he reaches the X on the map he can use the map to now find the actual buried treasure. If used indoors, the treasure is "hidden" rather than buried.

Best Age Group

6-10 years

Treasure Map Chart

Hamburger Chart

Materials
- poster board
- construction paper
- velcro

How to Make
- Cut several pieces of a hamburger and toppings out of construction paper (laminate if possible).
- Attach velcro to the back and to corresponding places on the chart.

How to Use
- Each time the child completes a desired task, a piece of the hamburger is put in place. When it is completely built a reward is given.

Best Age Group
6-10 years

Hamburger Chart

Clothesline Chart

Materials

- piece of string or yarn
- fabric scraps
- mini clothespins
- keep clothespins and clothes in a nearby basket

How to Make

- Hang some string across a wall or high up on a doorway.
- Cut various clothes out of scrap material.
- Keep clothespins and clothes in a nearby basket.

How to Use

- Throughout the day catch the child doing something positive. Each time he does, hang an article of clothing on the clothesline. When all of the clothes are hung on the line he receives an award.

Best Age Group

6-10 years

Bad Habit Chart

Materials

- poster board
- 2 litter bottle with top cut off (clear)
- scrap paper or old newspaper

How to Make

- Affix the 2 liter bottle to the poster board.
- Have scrap paper near the chart.

How to Use

- This chart is used to break a bad habit or decrease bad manners such as nose picking, not saying excuse me, etc. Each time the child does the unwanted behavior he crumples up a piece of scrap paper and throws it into the "trash can". The goal with this chart is to NOT let the trash can fill up. If he gets to the end of the day without filling up the trash, he receives a reward or privilege. The bottle can be cut smaller as he starts to decrease the habit.

Best Age Group

6-12 years

TRASH CAN

Hand Out Tickets

Materials

- roll of tickets or hand make

- paper

- markers

How to Make

- Make a sign that shows how many tickets needed to earn an item and hang in visible location.

How to Use

- As the child completes a desired task he is given a ticket. When enough tickets have been earned, he receives that reward.

Best Age Group

6-12 years

Hand Out Tickets

Movable Chart

Materials
- foam board or cork board
- paint
- one tack
- permanent marker (glitter optional)

How to Make
- Divide board into four sections.
- Paint each section a different color (add glitter to the top two).
- List 5 privileges in the first section, 4 privileges in the second section, 3 privileges in the third section, and 2 privileges in the last section.
- Draw 5 boxes in each section.
- Place tack in the top box on the chart.

How to Use
- Each color represents the amount of privileges the child has. For example, in the top color the child is free to do all available choices in that color during free times. Fewer choices are available in each section below one another. The tack represents the child. Each time he breaks a rule, he moves down a box. When he enters a new color, he's only allowed privileges in that color.

Best Age Group
Daily ages 7-10   Weekly ages 12 and up

Movable Chart

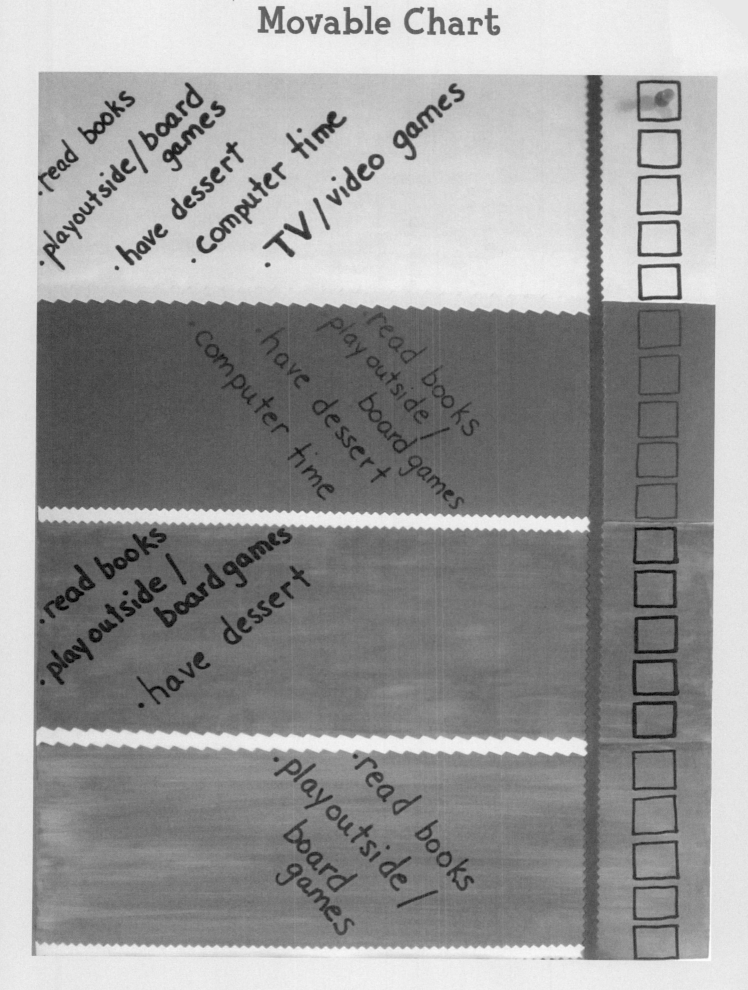

Bulls-Eye Chart

Materials

- poster board or cardboard
- paint or markers
- permanent marker

How to Make

- Cut a large circle out of cardboard or poster board.
- Paint to look like a dart board.
- Cut and paint a cardboard dart.
- Write in numbers with a permanent marker.

How to Use

- The child's dart starts at a number 5. Each time he completes a desired task he moves clockwise around the dartboard. When he reaches the "Bulls-Eye" he receives a reward.
- This can also be used as a level system similar to the "Moveable Chart". Place the dart on "50" which is the highest privilege zone. If there are unwanted behaviors he moves to the '25' zone where there are less privileges and so on. Restart each day in the '50' zone.

Best Age Group

7-12 years

Bulls-Eye Chart

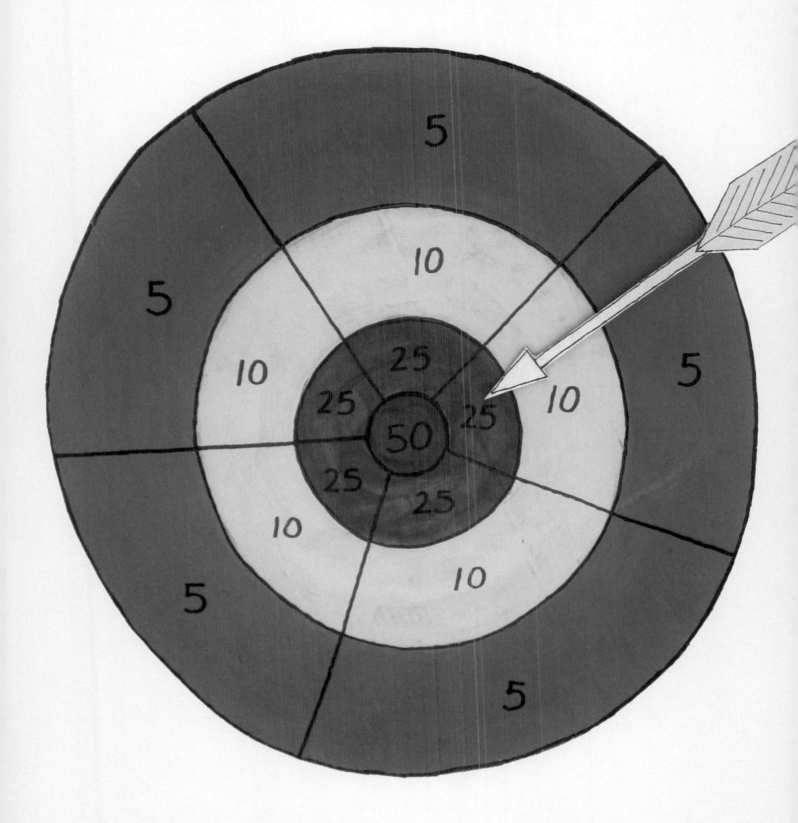

Timeline

Materials

- ruler or yardstick

- rubber band

    or

- hair band

How to Make

- Put a hair band or rubber band on the end of a ruler or yardstick.

How to Use

- Use a ruler with younger children and a yardstick with older children. Place the band starting at the very end of the stick. With each completed task, the rubber band moves to the next number. When the band reaches the end, a privilege is earned. This can also be used to track the number of chores or tasks left to complete.

Best Age Group

7-12 years

Timeline

Don't Get a Ticket Chart

Materials
- poster board
- markers
- white index cards
- copy paper

How to Make
- Cut a shape of a police officer's hat out of white copy paper and color.
- Attach it to a piece of poster board.
- Make several pockets out of copy paper and attach to the poster board.
- Write 'ticket' on each index card (enough for 1 per pocket).

How to Use
- Decide on a negative behavior that will be addressed. Each time the child demonstrates this particular behavior, he is given a ticket. If he exceeds the number of tickets allowed on the chart, he will lose a privilege.

Best Age Group
8-12 years

Don't Get a Ticket Chart

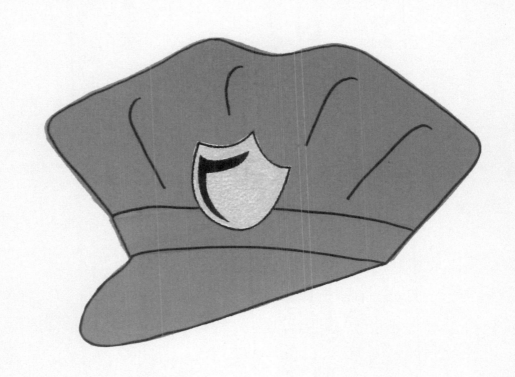

Tallymark Chart

Materials

- copy paper
- copier/printer
- outline of calendar for the month

How to Make

- Print out monthly calendar and divide each day into 4 sections.
- Make a key to represent what goal each section stands for.
- Make a key for privileges.

How to Use

- Each box per day represents four goals. Tally marks are given within each box at the end of the day depending on how well the task is carried out. Five tally marks is the highest; if the child does this task very well he receives five tally marks. If he does not complete the task it is a lower number or a zero. Marks are totaled at the end of the day and the key is used to determine the privilege for that day.

Best Age Group

10 and up

Tallymark Chart

AUGUST 2012

SUN	MON	TUE	WED	THU	FRI	SAT
||| || |||| ~~||||~~		**1**	**2**	**3**	**4**
~~||||~~ ~~||||~~ ||| ||						
5	**6**	**7**	**8**	**9**	**10**	**11**
12	**13**	**14**	**15**	**16**	**17**	**18**
19	**20**	**21**	**22**	**23**	**24**	**25**
26	**27**	**28**	**29**	**30**	**31**	

DAILY GOALS:

chores	home-work
be respectful	follow rules

Tally Mark key :

0-5 = read in room

6-10 = extended bedtime

11-15 = special privledge

16-20 = special activity

Fill In Chart

Materials

- copy paper
- printer or copy machine
- markers

How to Make

- Write out by hand or create on computer a weekly schedule with goals.
- It needs to be copied weekly.

How to Use

- Each day if the goal is completed the block can be filled in green. If it was not, it is filled in red. A number of green is decided upon to have filled in by the end of the week. If there are enough green boxes, a reward is given.

Best Age Group

10 and up

Fill In Chart

	SCHOOL WORK	COMPLETE CHORES	POSITIVE ATTITUDE	BE RESPECTFUL
SUN				
MON				
TUE				
WED				
THU				
FRI				
SAT				
TOTAL				

Earn Money Chart

Materials

- copy paper
- printer or copy machine

How to Make

- Create a weekly calendar with two big spaces for each day.

How to Use

- Each week a set amount of money will be given to the child. Throughout the week if he breaks a rule he will be given a deduction. It is written on the chart with the amount deducted. At the end of the week he totals the deductions and is given the balance. To keep him motivated, he can earn "bonus bucks" throughout the week. This can be an amount of money added to the day for extra work or a good deed.

Best Age Group

10 and up

Earn Money Chart

START $ _____

	DEACTIONS	BONUS BUCKS ★
SUN		
MON		
TUE		
WED		
THU		
FRI		
SAT		

FINISH $ _____

Even More

Create a small store in your house out of a clear plastic shoe organizer and small items the child likes. Each item should have its own price. Allow the child to earn play money and buy something at this store at the end of the day.

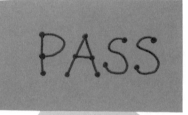

For kids who get up and down from the table or who are in and out of the house too much, give a "pass" that can be used only a certain number of times. This can be made by simply writing PASS on an index card. If the amount of times is exceeded, a privilege is taken away.

Allow the child to wear a special item such as a hair ribbon, watch, hat, etc., while he is showing the desired behavior. If he is not demonstrating required behavior, he will have to take off the item for a period of time.

BANK

Using magnetic money create a bank on the refrigerator. As the child earns money it is deposited in the bank. If rules are not being followed, money is withdrawn. The child can spend what is earned.

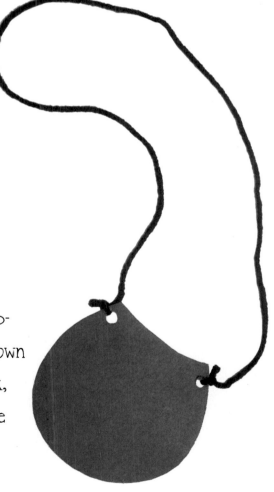

Wear a color coded necklace for phone interruptions and the like. When the color green is shown it is a talk time. When it is not a time to talk, simply turn it over to the red side. Reward the child when he responds to these visual cues.

Made in the USA
Middletown, DE
10 June 2018